25 Wacky & Wonderful STORIES THAT BOOST VOCABULARY

by Dan Greenberg

SCHOLASTIC PROFESSIONAL BOOKS

New York * Toronto * London * Auckland * Sydney
Mexico City * New Delhi * Hong Kong * Buenos Aires

Dedication

To my parents, Ruven and Julie,
who appreciate my efforts more than anyone.

Scholastic Inc. grants teachers permission to photocopy the reproducible pages from this book for classroom use. No other part of this publication may be reproduced in whole or in part, or stored in a retrieval system, or transmitted in any form or by any means, electronic, mechanical, photocopying, recording, or otherwise, without written permission of the publisher. For information regarding permission, write to Scholastic Inc., 555 Broadway, New York, NY 10012.

Cover design by Kelli Thompson
Interior design by Kelli Thompson
Cover and interior illustrations by Mike Moran
ISBN: 0-439-15586-X
Copyright © 2001 by Dan Greenberg
All rights reserved. Printed in the U.S.A.

TABLE OF CONTENTS

Introduction 5
Planning Skills Chart 6

Part 1: Just Prefixes

Rowena and Squirmy in "Bicycle Power" 8
Bill Klepper, Fat-Cat Wheeler-Dealer Billionaire 10
Bill Klepper, Fat-Head Wheeler-Dealer Billionaire 12

Part 2: Just Suffixes

Sufferin' Suffixes 16

Part 3: Affixes (Both Prefixes and Suffixes)

The Word Machine 20
Professor Sylvia's Word Values 23
Ancient Latin Quizmo!!! 25
The Cutting Edge 27
Nanette's Word Salon 29
Police Squad: MAU (Missing Affix Unit) 31

TABLE OF CONTENTS

Part 4: Build Your Vocabulary

Police Squad: SVU (Special Vocabulary Unit). 34

Emily Taproot's Poetry Workshop 36

Eddie Snively: World's Biggest Liar 38

Bingo Hackles, Sports Reporter. 40

The Four Vocabularians: Dr. Dialect's Dictionary of Deception. 42

Laverne Weaselford, U.S. Senator 44

Marla Murgatroid, Romance Novelist 45

Emily Taproot, Vocabulary Poet: The Language of Love 47

The Four Vocabularians: The National Word Day Speech 49

The Wordies 51

Buck Bickley's Big Braggin' Book 53

Buck Bickley's Dog's Braggin' Book 55

Julie Kablooie's Hollywood Gossip Column 56

Do You Have What It Takes to Become a Freelance Know-It-All Reviewer? . . . 57

Journey to a World Without Words. 59

Answers 61

Introduction

While most students have an innate fondness for learning and appreciating new words, this affinity often suffers when they are confronted with long, dry lists of isolated vocabulary words. *25 Wacky & Wonderful Stories That Boost Vocabulary* aims to remedy this unfortunate situation by putting vocabulary words into stories that are fun, friendly, and hilariously humorous.

In this book, your students will meet such characters as Bill Klepper, the prefix-buying billionaire, Aunt Aggie, who owns Aunt Aggie's Word Farm, The Four Vocabularians, Vocabulary Super-Heroes, and Buck Bickley, a world-class braggart and inventor of the famous Word Machine. They will also learn to associate learning new words as an opportunity for fun rather than an exercise in drudgery.

Special attention in the book is placed on the construction of words from simpler components. Prefixes and suffixes are attached to root words not only to show students how words are derived, but also to give students a strategy of how to break down unfamiliar words that they come across: *look at the prefixes and suffixes, find the root, compare it to other roots,* and so on. A handy **Planning Chart** is provided on page 6 to help organize word skills. Answers to the exercises are also given on pages 61-64.

Using The Book

The book is organized into four sections: Prefixes, Suffixes, Affixes (both prefixes and suffixes), and a Build Your Vocabulary section. Teachers who are especially interested in exposing students to word break-down strategies should complete the first three sections of the book first. Teachers who are less concerned with strategy may pick and choose lessons from any part of the book.

Guarantee

If you and your students don't get a chuckle out of these stories, the author, at no additional cost, will dip into his own *personal* collection of laughs, giggles, and chortles and supply you with a genuine chuckle that you are free to keep. Now there's an offer you can't refuse!

Planning Chart

Use this chart to select reproducible pages that will fit the individual needs of each student in your class.

Topic	Pages	Topic	Pages
Number prefixes: mono-, uni-, bi-, di-, du-, tri-, quad-, tetra-, quint-, hex-, sept-, oct-, non-, dec-, deci-, cent-, centi-, kilo-, milli-, mega-, poly-, multi-	8, 9	**Where prefixes:** a-, ac- ad-, ab-, be-, circum-, con-, contro-, de-, dia-, di-, en-, em-, epi-, ex-, extra-, extro-, hyper-, im-, in-, inter-, intro-, ob-, over-, para-, per-, pro-, sub-, super-, tele-, trans-	8, 9, 12, 13, 20, 21, 22, 23, 24, 25, 26, 27, 28, 29, 30, 31, 32
Not prefixes: a-, dis-, ig-, il-, un-, im-, in-, ir-, mis-	10, 11, 20, 21, 22, 27, 28	**Together prefixes:** co-, con-, cor-, syn-, sym-	10, 11, 27, 28, 29, 30
When prefixes: pre-, post-, re-	12, 13, 20, 21, 22, 27, 28, 29, 30	**Miscellaneous prefixes:** geo-	31, 32
Adjective suffixes: -al, -ant, -ate, -ful, -ial, -less, -ous, -ian, -ible, -ic, -ile, -ive, -y	16, 17, 20, 21, 22, 25, 26, 27, 28, 29, 30	**Noun suffixes:** -able, -ability, -age, -ation, -ator, -er, -ier, -ition, -ion, -logue, -ment, -ology, -or, -ory, -ty, -ize, -ure	16, 17, 20, 21, 22, 23, 24, 25, 26, 27, 28, 29, 30, 31, 32
Root words: neo, nov, ann, enn	51, 52	**Context clues**	34, 35, 36, 37, 38, 39, 42, 43, 44, 45, 46, 52, 53, 54, 57, 58, 59, 60
Antonyms	45, 46	**Synonyms**	40, 41, 45, 46, 47, 48, 49, 50, 55, 56, 59, 60

PART 1

Just Prefixes

Name _____ Date _____

Rowena and Squirmy in "Bicycle Power"

> Knock, knock.
> Who's there?
> Weirdo.
> Weirdo who?
> Weirdo you think you're going on that shiny new bicycle?
> Beats me.

The prefix **bi-** is a number word that tells you how many wheels a bicycle has. What do you think **bi-** means?

Number Prefixes: Some prefixes stand for numbers

- A **bi**cycle has two wheels.
- A **tri**cycle has three wheels.

How often would **bi**weekly be?

How many outs do you make in a **tri**ple play?

How many centuries are in a **bi**centennial?

Here are some other prefixes that define numbers, amounts, or ideas.

Prefixes: Numbers, Amounts, and Ideas

Prefix	Meaning of Prefix	Prefix	Meaning of Prefix
mono-, uni-	one	non-	nine
bi-, di-, du-	two	dec-, deci-	ten, tenth
tri-	three	cent-, centi-	hundred, hundredth
quad-, tetra-	four	kilo-, milli-	thousand, thousandth
quint-	five	mega-	million, large
hex-	six	poly-, multi-	many
sept-	seven	hyper-, over-, extra-, super-	above, beyond, more, greater
oct-	eight		

Circle the definition for each boldfaced word.

1. Rowena rode a **unicycle** to town to see the Woovis Comedy Show.
   a. bike without wheels   **b.** one-wheeled bike   **c.** a single circle

2. As a **biannual** event, the Comedy Show was returning to the Bow-Wow Theater for the first time in two years.
   a. once every two years   **b.** once a year   **c.** twice a year

8

Name _____   Date _____

3. Squirmy set up his camera on a **tripod** to take pictures of the show.
   a. three-legged camera stand   **b.** four-lens camera   **c.** three-legged camera
4. Woovis has been perfecting his comedy routine for an entire **decade**.
   a. ten dollars   **b.** five-year period   **c.** ten-year period
5. Woovis performed his comedy **monologue** alone on stage.
   a. one-person speech   **b.** two-person show   **c.** group speech

Complete each sentence.

6. If a **decagon** is a ten-sided figure, a **hexagon** is a _____.
7. If a **biped** is a two-legged organism, a **quadruped** is a _____.
8. A **kilobyte** has _____ units of computer memory called "bytes."
9. A **megabyte** has a _____ units of computer memory called "bytes."
10. A **polytechnic** school offers studies in _____ technical fields.

GOING BEYOND

Can you think of a good name for a six-wheeled cycle? Make up a word. Then use the prefixes on this page to make up the words below. Note that the words you make up may or may not actually exist.

1. a bicycle that has five wheels _____
2. a thousand-pound hamster _____
3. a three-point basket in a basketball game _____
4. a car that costs one-million dollars _____

Name _____ Date _____

> MY NAME IS SASHA DASH. SO YOU THINK YOUR BOSS IS **ATYPICAL**? YOU SEEM TO **MISINTERPRET** EVERYTHING HE OR SHE SAYS? THEN TRY WORKING FOR . . .

Bill Klepper, Fat-Cat Wheeler-Dealer Billionaire

At 9:00 sharp I walked into the office. "Good morning," I said. Bill Klepper didn't answer. I tried again. "Good morning!"

"Dash," he said, "I've decided to do away with *good morning* in this office. It wastes time and money. Do you realize that in the space of a single 'good morning' I could've earned over 32 thousand dollars?!"

"Amazing," I said.

"You're absolutely right it's amazing," he said. "Now let's get to work. I want you to buy PREFIXES today."

"Prefixes?" I asked. "Aren't those the little things that come at the front of words?"

"That's right," he said. "And we're going to buy them up until there's a huge **imbalance** in the market. That way, every time someone uses a prefix—they'll need to pay ME a royalty."

I couldn't **disagree** with the basic idea. It might be **ignoble**, but it was clever. Devilishly clever.

I made a list of NOT prefixes (prefixes that mean "no" or "not"). In theory, you should be able to combine prefixes and root words to make new words. But would it work?

To find out, complete the exercises. And keep in mind that Bill Klepper owns these prefixes. Every time you use one, he gets a big fat KICKBACK.

"Not" Prefixes

a–	im–
dis–	in–
ig–	ir–
il–	mis–
un–	

Root Words

noble
balance
popular
typical
exact
agree
interpret
literate
responsible

Name _____ Date _____

Bill Klepper, Fat-Cat

Use the root words from page 10 and the definitions in parentheses to make each word.

1. a- + root = _____ (not average)
2. dis- + root = _____ (not share the same opinion)
3. ig- + root = _____ (not respectable)
4. il- + root = _____ (not able to read)
5. im- + root = _____ (not the same on both sides)
6. in- + root = _____ (not precise)
7. ir- + root = _____ (not dependable)
8. mis- + root = _____ (fail to understand)
9. un- + root = _____ (not well liked)

We started simple, with just a few prefixes.

Then we kept buying more and more of them. You can use these prefixes with the root words shown to make new words. But keep in mind: *if a word has a prefix, then Bill Klepper will someday own it!*

"Together" Prefixes

co-   cor-
con-   sym-
syn-

More Root Words

metric
exist
thesis
descend
respond

Use the root words on this page and the definitions in parentheses to write each word.

10. co- + root = _____ (be alive together)
11. con- + root = _____ (go down together to a lower level)
12. cor- + root = _____ (answer one another by writing)
13. sym- + root = _____ (balanced on both sides by measurement)
14. syn- + root = _____ (the combining of different things or ideas)

According to my calculations, we'll make millions on this, perhaps even billions. In fact, don't be surprised if in a few years *BILL KLEPPER HAS ALL THE MONEY IN THE WORLD!* It could happen. Stay tuned.

GOING BEYOND

Using the new vocabulary words from this activity, write a letter to Mr. Klepper telling what you think of his scheme.

Name _____ Date _____

Bill Klepper, Fat Head

I'M SASHA DASH. DO FINANCIAL TRANSACTIONS TURN YOU ON? IF SO, YOU'VE COME TO THE RIGHT PLACE. BECAUSE, YOU SEE, I DON'T WORK FOR JUST ANYBODY. I WORK FOR...

Bill Klepper, Fat-~~Cat~~ Head Wheeler-Dealer Billionaire

One Tuesday morning Mr. Klepper called me into his office.

"Dash, take a look at my head," he said. "Does it look abnormal? It feels like I'm wearing a beach ball on top of my neck!"

Bill Klepper's been doing so much wheeling and dealing lately that his head's starting to swell.

"Looks okay to me," I lied.

"Good," he said. "Let's get to work. I want you to buy more prefixes today."

"More prefixes?" I asked. "We just bought dozens of prefixes yesterday. Why are you so preoccupied with prefixes?"

"I just like to adjoin one word to another," he explained. "Today I want you to get me all of the WHERE and WHEN prefixes."

"No problem," I sighed.

In my subconscious I know that this will be no simple task. Look at how many WHERE and WHEN prefixes there are—too many! Notice that some of the same prefixes appear both here and on pages 10 and 11. But the prefixes have DIFFERENT meanings! This could imperil our ability to tell one word from another.

But Klepper says "no problem." As long as we use the prefix chart below, we should be able to make all the words we need.

Where Prefixes	Meaning of Prefix	Where Prefixes	Meaning of Prefix
a-, ac-, ad-	on, toward, to	im-, en-, em-	into, cause to be
ab-	off, away	para-, trans-	along, beside, beyond
be-	over, around	sub-	under
circum-	around	dia-, di-	through, across
ex-	out	inter-	between
When Prefixes	Meaning of Prefix	When Prefixes	Meaning of Prefix
pre-	before	re-	again, back
post-	after		

Bill Klepper, Fat Head

Name _____ Date _____

Circle the meaning of the boldfaced word. Use the prefix meanings in the chart to help you.

1. Trouble is **afoot** whenever Bill Klepper gets one of his BIG ideas. (a- + foot)
   a. off your foot   b. oncoming   c. on your foot

2. Klepper's latest BIG idea is to **adjoin** prefixes to other words. (ad- + join)
   a. attach to   b. become a member   c. not attach

3. Klepper's enemies think his ideas are **abnormal**. (ab- + normal)
   a. very average   b. away from typical   c. ordinary

4. Klepper would just as soon **exterminate** his enemies. (ex- + terminate)
   a. tease   b. help   c. get rid of

5. As for myself—I have **endeared** myself to Klepper. (en- + dear)
   a. made available   b. caused to be a deer   c. caused to be loved

6. We have become **interdependent** — Klepper needs me, and I need him. (inter- + dependent)
   a. separate   b. not dependent   c. depend on each other

7. Klepper depends on me to make his financial **transactions**. (trans- + action)
   a. big gains   b. not active   c. events between people

8. I do so many things for Klepper that it is almost impossible to **circumscribe** the duties of my job. (circum- + scribe)
   a. run in circles   b. draw a line around   c. expand

9. But every time that I ask Klepper for a raise, I feel that I am **imperiling** my job. (im- + peril)
   a. putting in danger   b. understanding   c. making fun of

10. Klepper claims to have **paranormal** abilities when it comes to making money. (para- + normal)
    a. beyond ordinary   b. funny   c. poor

11. Even Klepper's **subconscious** mind is filled with schemes to make money. (sub- + conscious)
    a. asleep   b. underground   c. just below thinking

12. On the phone, Klepper gave me a **preview** of his money philosophy. (pre + view)
    a. a look before   b. a look after   c. a long look

13. "Money **regenerates** the spirit," Klepper explained. (re- + generates)
    a. replaces   b. gives birth to again   c. runs down

14. "Money also **becalms** me," said Klepper (be- + calms)
    a. surround by calm   b. surround   c. make nervous

GOING BEYOND

Now, Klepper has a new task. Find the prefixes in the chart that we *didn't* use in the exercises above. Then look up a word in the dictionary for each one. Are you up to it? Go ahead and give it a try.

13

PART 2

Just Suffixes

Name _____ Date _____

Sufferin' Suffixes

Greetings from America's Heartland! This is Aunt Aggie, reporting to you from Aunt Aggie's Down Home **Word Farm**! My Word Farm is just like any other farm. 'Cept for one thing—instead of cows and chickens, I raise **WORDS**.

That's right, on Aunt Aggie's Farm we raise 100 percent grain-fed Government Inspected and Approved Words. Why, over on the south forty, I've got a crop of adjectives and prepositions comin' up right now. Cute little sprouts, they are.

Then, on the north forty we've got your homonyms and synonyms. Hard to tell 'em apart sometimes.

And down by the river we've got your passwords, watchwords, and catchwords, bordered by some nifty rows of stuff and nonsense.

But stuff and nonsense ain't what I'm here to tell ya about today. Nope, I'm here to tell ya about my Sufferin' Suffixes.

Turns out, no matter what you do with these things, no matter how carefully you plant 'em, water 'em, and tend 'em, they still end up comin' **AFTER** all the other words. Here's a whole list of 'em.

Suffix	Meaning of Suffix	Suffix	Meaning of Suffix
-able, -ability	capable of	-ful, -ous	full of
-age, -ty	action, state of, collection	-ian	person who is, does
-al	of, relating to, resembling	-ic, -ory	characterized by
-ant	something or someone that is	-ize	to make or become this way
-ate	having the quality of	-less	without
-ation, -ition, -ion	the act of, result of	-ment	result of action or process
-er, -ier, -or	something or someone that does		

Each suffix always comes after other words (or parts of words). And there's nothin' you can do about it.

Name _____ **Date** _____

Add a suffix from the box to each boldfaced root to make a word that matches the definition. Use a dictionary to check each word.

1. Capable of being received or **accept**ed _____

2. The act of adjusting or **adapt**ing to something _____

3. Without **heed**ing, or without being mindful of _____

4. A doctor who works in a **clinic** _____

5. In court, someone who is accused, and must **defend** him or herself _____

6. Full of **wonder** _____

7. Full of scorn, or **disdain** _____

8. Resembling false visions, or **delusion**s _____

9. Result of having a right to something, or **entitle**d _____

10. Connected by the state of being **marri**ed _____

11. Characterized by **poet**ry _____

12. To affirm the legality of, or **valid**ity _____

13. To use **digit**al information to make _____

14. Something that holds back, or **inhibits** _____

GOING BEYOND
Some words, like **helplessness** or **childishness**, have two suffixes. Can you think of another word that has two suffixes?

PART 3

Affixes

(Both Prefixes and Suffixes)

The Word Machine

Name _____ Date _____

An Interview With Buck Bickley, Inventor of
THE WORD MACHINE
by Laverne "Sparky" LaVeque

Sparky: I'm Laverne "Sparky" LaVeque, reporter for *The Daily Blab*. Today I'm interviewing Buck Bickley, the Inventor of the Word Machine. Tell us about yourself, Buck.

Buck: I'm Buck Bickley, the Smartest Guy on Earth. I'm also the inventor of the Word Machine.

Sparky: Wow, the Smartest Guy on Earth, that's impressive.

Buck: Absolutely! Go ahead and ask me something. Anything.

Sparky: Okay. What's the capital of Oklahoma?

Buck: That would be . . . Denver.

Sparky: No.

Buck: Kansas City? No, wait—I've got it. Sacramento. Sacramento is the capital of Oklahoma.

Sparky: Actually, it's Oklahoma City.

Buck: Dad-blast it! I'm so mad I could...

Sparky: Let's get back to the Word Machine. How does it work?

20

Name _____ Date _____

Buck: This I know about. You put **prefixes** in here. **Suffixes** here. And **roots** here. And *voila*! Out comes a brand-spanking-new word, suitable for writing, speaking, or even storing in the freezer like a frozen peanut-butter sandwich. For example, right now we have the root SPECT loaded in the Word Machine. SPECT means "to look."

Sparky: So what happens?

Buck: A prefix like *re-*, *ex-*, or *in-* is put on the front. Then, a suffix like *-able* or *-ful* is added in the back. Then, step back, out comes the word! *Respectful*. It means to be full of respect or appreciation for something or someone.

Sparky: Wow, that looks like fun! May I try it?

Buck: Sure.

THE WORD MACHINE

Use the prefixes or suffixes given below to form the defined words.

Definition	Prefix	Root	Suffix
1. To look inward closely		SPECT	
2. To look outward for the possibility that something will happen		(S)PECT	
3. Someone who looks at an event		SPECT	
4. Being careful by looking all around		SPECT	
5. Something that one looks forward to		SPECT	
6. A thorough view, most likely		SPECT	
7. People give this when they "look again" at someone and show their appreciation		SPECT	
8. Someone who does not "look again" or show appreciation is full of this		RESPECT	

Prefixes

circum- = around   dis- = not   ex- = out   in- = in
pro- = forward   re- = again   per- = thorough, through

Suffixes

-ful = full of   -ive = likely to be   -ator, -or = one who does

Name _____ **Date** _____

Sparky: Wow, this is super fun! Can we use the Word Machine to make more words?

Buck: Sure, you can make oodles of different words.

Add both prefixes and suffixes from page 21 to the root *spect* to make words for these definitions.

9. The act of looking closely at something _____

10. Someone who looks closely and carefully at something _____

GOING BEYOND

Use the Word Machine to make up your own word. Write a dictionary entry for your new word.

Name _____ Date _____

Professor Sylvia's Word Values

Dear Fellow Word Collectors,

If you're like me, words are your life. You've got them scattered all over your house, and you're always wondering how much the darn things are worth. Well, wonder no more! Thanks to my fabulous new Word-O-Matic computer software, I can now find the market value of ANY word in the English language. So send me your words!

Sincerely yours,

Professor Sylvia Palabra

Use the prefixes, suffixes, and definitions in the box to complete each letter.

"Port" Words (to carry)	Prefixes	Suffixes
deportment: manner in which one carries oneself	**de-**: out of	**-able**: capable of
importer: person who ships goods from other countries	**im-**: into	**-age**: action
portage: to carry over land	**trans-**: across	**-er**: one who does
portable: able to be carried easily		**-ment**: process
transport: to move from place to place		

LETTER #1

Dear Professor Sylvia,
While rummaging through the back alley behind my house, I stumbled across the root **port**. What a find! I added a prefix that means "across" to jazz it up a little. What word did I end up with? What does it mean and how much is it worth?

Signed, Back Alley Rummager

Dear Rum:
Nice find! The word you made is (1) _____.
It means _____.
The value of your word? Well, it's a fabulous word, don't get me wrong. But even in top condition it's not worth much more than 34 cents.
Better luck next time,
Professor Sylvia

Name _____ Date _____

Professor Sylvia

LETTER #2

Dear Professor Sylvia,
I was at a mall, buying French words, when the seller threw this word in as a freebie. It uses the root **port** but I lost both the prefix and the suffix. It describes someone who sends things from France to the U.S.A. What is this word and how much is it worth?

Signed, Curious and Greedy

Dear Curious: The word you received is (2) _____. It means _____.

In perfect condition, with the original prefix, this word might be worth over 12 thousand dollars! However, as is, the word is valued only at about 34 cents.
Too bad!
Professor Sylvia

LETTER #3

Dear Sylvia,
My Aunt Charlene gave me the root word **port** for my twelfth birthday. I wanted a scooter. It's got a prefix and a suffix and it describes how you carry yourself. How much can I get for it? I need to sell it for enough money to buy a scooter.

Signed, Scooterless

Dear Scoot: The word you received is (3) _____. It means _____.

This word fetched prices of over $50,000 before it got popular. Then it started popping up everywhere and its value dropped. Unfortunately, its current value is no more than 34 cents.
Looks like you'll be walking,
Professor Sylvia

LETTER #4

Dear Professor Sylvia,
I found the root word **port** on my pillow in Room 306 of a Yesterday Inn in Sioux City, Iowa. Someone told me that it's valuable and it means something like you can carry me around. Can you help me?

Signed, Sioux City Sue

Dear Sue:
The word you received does have a meaning that is similar to "carry around easily." It is the word (4) _____. It means _____.

In Japan, this word goes for the astronomical price of 60 billion yen. However, since you got it in Iowa, its value drops down to a little less than 34 cents.
Hey, what can you do, Sue?
Professor Sylvia

GOING BEYOND

Make a new word by adding a prefix *pro-* and a suffix *-ion* to *port*. Now add the prefix *dis-* to your new word to form a second word. Finally, add the suffix *-able* to the second word to form a third word. Use a dictionary to define the three words and then use them in sentences.

Ancient Latin Quizmo

Name _____ Date _____

HEY, GANG, PUT ON YOUR TOGAS AND GET READY, BECAUSE IT'S TIME TO PLAY . . .

Ancient Latin Quizmo!!!

Ject (to throw)	Script, Scribe (to write)
$C ($100)	$C ($100)
$CC ($200)	$CC ($200)
$CCC ($300)	$CCC ($300)
$LD ($400)	$LD ($400)
$D ($500)	$D ($500)

Murray: I'm your host, Murray Titus Andronicus, also known as "Murray the T." And now it's time to meet our fabulous contestants. First, say "hello" to Emily Taproot! This little powerhouse of a classical poet has had three smash hit poems and two hot-selling dirges over the last six centuries alone. [applause]

Emily: It's great to be here, Murray. In fact, you could sort of say, it's *classic*.

Murray: And now let me introduce, from the good old USA, ace reporter Laverne "Sparky" La Veque. [applause]

Sparky: Thank you, Murray. Thank you. It's always great to be here.

Murray: And finally, he's known as the World's Smartest Guy, none other than the inventor of the Word Machine himself, Mr. Buck Bickley. [applause]

Buck: Go ahead and ask me something, Murray. Anything. Go ahead.

Murray: Okay, Buck. From what ancient culture do we get the Latin roots for the words in today's game?

Buck: That would be Baltimore, Murray. Baltimore, Maryland.

Murray: No, we get our Latin roots from the ancient culture of Rome. Rome, Italy. Rome and Baltimore are over 8,000 miles apart. Now, let's play Quizmo! Buck, what category would you like?

Buck: I'll take JECT for 100 dollars, Murray.

Murray: This word means "to throw out." It uses the root *ject* and a prefix that means "out." What is it?

Buck: Uh, is it the singer Michael *Jection*, Murray?

Murray: No, Buck. That would be wrong.

Emily: I'll take a chance here. Is it *eject*, Murray? [DING DING DING!]

Murray: Correctimundo, Emily [applause]. Select again.

Emily: JECT for $200.

Sparky: Let's give our home audience a chance to play the game.

Murray: That's a great idea, Sparky. In fact, here are more of the clues from today's game.

Ancient Latin Quizmo

Name _____ Date _____

Use the prefixes and suffixes in the box to answer each question.

Prefixes and Suffixes

Prefix	Meaning	Suffix	Meaning
de-	out; take out of	-ile	of, relating to, capable of
ob-	against, toward	-able	able to
in-	in, into	-ure	condition of
sub-	under	-ive	likely to be
con-	with	-ion	state or quality of
circum-	around		

1. **JECT FOR $200:** Attach an "in" prefix and a suffix that means "the state of" to **ject** and get something that the doctor sticks in your arm. What is it? _____

2. **JECT FOR $300:** Start with the root **ject**. Attach a prefix that means "against," and a suffix that means "likely to be." The word means to be "fair, unbiased, and to see without a slant." What is it? _____

3. **JECT FOR $400:** Attach a prefix that means "under" to **ject** and the same suffix as in word number 2 to get a word that means "not affected by the outer world." What is the word? _____

4. **JECT FOR $500:** Stick a "forward" prefix and a "relating to" suffix onto the root **ject** to get a word that describes something that zooms through the air like a missile. Wow! What is it? _____

5. **SCRIB FOR $100:** Attach an "in" prefix to **scribe** to get a word that means "to write or carve in an official way." What is it? _____

6. **SCRIPT FOR $200:** Attach a "with" prefix to **script** and get "someone who is forced to serve." Who is it? _____

7. **SCRIB FOR $300:** Attach two prefixes—the first "in;" the second "out"—to scrib, then attach a "capable of" suffix and get a word that is impossible to tell about. What is it? _____

8. **FINAL QUIZMO: JECT FOR $1000:** This word is just a "guess." It has a "with" prefix and a "condition of" suffix. Can you "guess" what it is and what it means? _____

GOING BEYOND

Choose two words that you wrote above and use them to write two Quizmo questions on any subject. Exchange papers with a partner and answer the questions.

The Cutting Edge

Name _____ Date _____

Prefixes and Suffixes

Prefix or Suffix	Meaning	Prefix or Suffix	Meaning
pre-	before	ex-	away from
con-	together	inter-	to each other
de-	reduce	-ion	result of
dis-	remove	-or	something that does
in-	into	-ive	inclined to

The prefixes and suffixes above were added to the roots *cis* and *sect* to make the Cutting Edge Words below.

Cutting Edge Words

cis: to cut or kill
- **concise**: clear and short in words
- **decisive**: draws strong conclusions
- **incisive**: clear, sharp, full of insight
- **precision**: accuracy
- **incision**: a cut made by a doctor

sect: to cut
- **dissect**: to cut up a body for studying
- **intersect**: to cross; when two things (roads) cross each other
- **cross-section**: a sample of a population
- **sector**: part or division

Fill in each blank with the Cutting Edge words below.

My name is Laverne "Sparky" LaVeque. You probably know me by my pen name, *Dr. Sparky*. No, I'm not that kind of doctor. I don't make **(1)** [surgical cuts] _____ or do medical operations.

Instead, you could call me a "doctor of words." I write a column for the *Daily Blab*. Hey, I might as well say it, *I'm good*. I'm also tough, thoughtful, and **(2)** [insightful] _____. Each day, I **(3)** [cut apart] _____ every **(4)** [region] _____ of the news with great care and **(5)** [exactness] _____.

The Cutting Edge

Name _____ Date _____

To make a long story more **(6)** [to the point] _____, until yesterday everything was going great. Readers seemed to love me. So did my editor. Hey, even my cat loved me, and he doesn't even know how to read!

In fact, the only person around here who didn't seem to be on my side was George Barrett Gaspar III, the publisher of this paper. (We call him "Gasbags.") Here's the memo that Gasbags wrote to my editor:

"I want to **(7)** [cut] _____ Dr. X from the paper. She doesn't reach a **(8)** [variety of people] _____ of our audience. She's not **(9)** [conclusive] _____. Her interests do not **(10)** [cross each other] _____ with those of the typical reader. She's just not enough on the 'cutting edge.'

In order to save my job, please help me correct my Cutting Edge problems by answering the following questions.

11. What are the prefixes for the words **excise** and **incisive**? What does each word have to do with cutting? _____
_____

12. The word **bisect** means "to cut in two." What does the word trisect mean?
_____
_____

13. An **incisor** is a kind of tooth. What kind of tooth do you suppose an **incisor** is—sharp? Dull? What animals have **incisor** teeth?
_____
_____

Thanks! Look for my column in tomorrow's issue of the *Daily Blab*.

Signed — *Dr. Sparky*

GOING BEYOND
Choose any of the words on this page. Write a story that explains how the word came to have its meaning.

Name _____   Date _____

Nanette's Word Salon

Nanette: Hello, and welcome to Nanette's Word Salon. I'm Nanette, your host. How can I help you today?

Customer: Do you carry words that use the **vert** or **vers** root?

Nanette: We certainly do. In fact, we're running a special sale on **vert** and **vers** words today: buy one, get one free. Incidentally, the roots **vert** and **vers** mean "to turn."

Customer: Excellent. Let me explain what I need. I'm going to make some changes in my life. So I was thinking of a **vert** word that means "to change."

Nanette: Did you have any special prefix or suffix in mind?

Customer: A prefix, perhaps. Something simple. No suffixes. They make the word too long. It gives me a headache sometimes.

Nanette: I think I've got the perfect word for you. It's called **convert**. It means "to change" and it has a simple prefix and no suffix.

Customer: Do you think it will fit me?

Nanette: Go ahead and try it out. There's no extra charge.

Customer: The bank will *convert* Italian money into American dollars. Why, yes! Oh, I love it. How much will that be?

Nanette: Aren't you forgetting something—the two-for-one sale?

Customer: But I really don't need any other words.

Nanette: Look, why don't you just try one out? I know you don't like suffixes, but—

Customer: What do you have in mind?

Nanette: Perhaps attaching a simple "-ible" to **convert** to give you the word **convertible**. What do you think?

Customer: [gushing] Oh my goodness! That's so clever. I can't believe it was that easy. Can you really do that?

Nanette: Why not? Go ahead and try it out.

Customer: A *convertible* car can change its roof. I don't think I've ever enjoyed a word with a suffix so much. How can I ever thank you?

Nanette: You can help me assemble some of these other **vert** and **vers** words.

Nanette's Word Salon

Name _____ Date _____

Prefixes and Suffixes

Prefix or Suffix	Meaning	Prefix or Suffix	Meaning
in-	into	extro-	outward
re-	again, back	contro-	capable of
con-	with	-ial	relating to
sub-	under	-y	against
intro-	inward	-ible	condition of
		-ion, -ation	act of, result of

Write the word to answer each question. Use the prefixes and suffixes in the box to help you.

1. Like to be upside down? Attach an "into" prefix to **verse** and get an upside-down word. What word do you get? _____

2. Perhaps you're tired of being upside down. Go back to what you were by attaching an "again" prefix to **verse**. What word do you get? _____

3. Attach a "result of" suffix to the words you wrote for questions 1–2 and get two words that mean "the result of" those words. What are they? (Note: take off the "e" at the end of each word before adding the suffix.) _____

4. This is a nasty word that digs underneath something and causes damage. Get it by attaching an "under" prefix to **vert**. What is it? _____

5. Knock off the "t" at the end of the word you wrote for question 4 and replace it with an "s." Attach a "result of" suffix to describe a treacherous act. What is it? _____

6. Here's a shy word. You need to coax it to come forward by attaching a prefix that means "inward" to **vert**. What is the word? _____

7. This word is the opposite of shy. It's friendly and outgoing. You get it by attaching a prefix that means "outward" to **vert**. What is it? _____

8. This word is liable to cause an argument. You get it by attaching an "against" prefix and a "condition of" suffix to **vers**. Don't argue. Just write what it is. _____

9. Replace the suffix at the end of the word you wrote for question 8 with a "relating to" suffix. Now you have a word that describes issues that start arguments. What is the word? _____

GOING BEYOND

Write a definition for each word you made on this page. Then look up the words in the dictionary. How do your definitions compare?

Name _____ Date _____

> MY NAME IS RALPH EDGE. I'M A POLICE OFFICER. BUT NOT JUST ANY COP. I'M A MEMBER OF . . .

Police Squad: MAU

Police Squad: MAU (Missing Affix Unit)

In the Missing Affix Unit we hunt down missing prefixes and suffixes. These are real cases. Here are some actual calls we got just today. Match one of the affixes below to each caller.

NOTE: IF ONE OF YOUR PREFIXES OR SUFFIXES IS MISSING CALL 555-MISS

Possible Missing Prefixes & Suffixes

geo-   tele-   trans-   -ation   -logue   -ology

Help Ralph Edge find Steve Ranger's missing prefix for the numbered blanks. Then use the prefix to complete all of the numbered words.

CALL 1: 8:54 A.M., TUESDAY
CALLER'S NAME: STEVE RANGER, BIG-SHOT TV PRODUCER

TRANSCRIPT OF THE CALL: This is Steve Ranger, big-shot TV producer. About an hour ago something strange happened. I was in the middle of filming a TV show when suddenly we lost our prefix. At first, all I noticed was that the **(1)** _____ phones weren't ringing. Then I turned on the **(2)** _____ vision. Nothing was working. I was supposed to **(3)** _____ vise a **(4)** _____ play that I wrote. Everything was set up, including the **(5)** _____ communications equipment and the **(6)** _____ photo cameras. If I don't find this prefix, the entire **(7)** _____ cast will be ruined! Can you help me?

31

Name _____ Date _____

Help Ralph Edge find Suzie Chuckles' missing suffix for the numbered blanks. Then use the suffix to complete all of the numbered words.

CALL 2: 12:45 P.M., TUESDAY
CALLER'S NAME: SUZIE CHUCKLES, COMEDIAN

TRANSCRIPT OF THE CALL: My name is Suzie Chuckles and I need your help. I'm a comedian, but this isn't funny. I was working on my **(8)** mono_____ when I lost my suffix. Hey, I can't just look in a **(9)** cata_____ and order jokes. I have this continuing **(10)** dia_____ with my agent about suffixes. He says suffixes don't matter. I say suffixes do matter. Now look what's happened! Without this suffix my act is ruined. Can you help me?

Help Ralph Edge find Louie Blozzáy's missing prefix for the numbered blanks. Then use the prefix to complete all of the numbered words.

CALL 3: 4:06 P.M., TUESDAY
CALLER'S NAME: LOUIE BLOZZÁY, SCIENTIST

TRANSCRIPT OF THE CALL: This is Professor Louie Blozzáy, calling from somewhere outside Inner Mongomia. Or perhaps I'm inside Outer Mongomia. Let me explain. I am a **(11)**_____physicist and I study the physical processes of Earth. I've been looking for **(12)**_____logical clues about Earth's past. I was hot on the trail of sparkling **(13)**_____odes inside a steamy **(14)**_____thermic volcano when I made a few mistakes in **(15)**_____graphy and suddenly realized that I was lost and I had lost a prefix. Can you help me (a) figure out where I am, and (b) find the missing prefix? Thank you very much.

GOING BEYOND

Check out the definition of each of your words in a dictionary. Then, write a definition for each prefix and suffix you used.

Police Squad: MAU

32

PART 4

Build Your Vocabulary

Name _____ **Date** _____

MY NAME IS BETTY STOKES. I'M A POLICE OFFICER. BUT NOT JUST ANY COP. I'M A MEMBER OF...

Police Squad: SVU (Special Vocabulary Unit)

In the SVU, we solve cases that involve words. If you're a word, you'd better know who I am. Because if you start trouble, you'll see me. I'll be your worst nightmare. I'll be in your face faster than a freshly laundered pillowcase at bedtime.

8:46 P.M., Saturday We got a call over on 13th Street. There was a **big fight**. We hauled in five suspects. They all said, "It wasn't me." But that's what they always say. One of them wasn't telling the truth. So we put them in a lineup. Here are their stories:

Each suspect is a word from the Word List. Write the word that fits into each blank space.

Word List

affront: to insult intentionally

altercation: a bitter argument
animosity: open hatred
confrontation: a face-off

felony: a serious crime such as murder, assault, or rape

fracas: a noisy, disorderly brawl
skirmish: a small, early battle
trespass: to go into forbidden territory

Suspect Word #1: Look at me. Do I look like a fight? I'm not a fight. I may be the attitude that starts fights. But I'm not the fight itself. So I'm not your word.

(1) _____

Suspect Word #2: All right, I'll admit. I am a kind of a fight. But not the big fight you're looking for. I'm more of a small fight, just the beginning battle in a larger war. So I'm not the one you're looking for. (2) _____

Name _____ Date _____

Police Squad: SVU

Suspect Word #3: This is all I'll say: I'm big. I'm noisy and disorderly. Some people call me a brawl. But I wasn't anywhere near 13th Street. So it couldn't have been me. **(3)** _____

Suspect Word #4: When you boil it all down, I'm nothing more than an argument. An argument is not really a fight. So it isn't me. **(4)** _____

Suspect Word #5: I could be sort of a fight. But really, I'm more of a face-to-face meeting that could lead to a fight. So it isn't me. **(5)** _____

Which one did Betty think was the big fight? Explain why you chose that suspect.
_____
_____

11:54 P.M., Saturday: No sooner did we get that cleaned up, than we got a call from Avenue G. It appeared that a serious crime had been committed. We rounded up the usual assortment of suspects and took down their stories. Only one of them is really a serious crime.

Suspect Word #1: I'm nothing more than walking in the wrong place at the wrong time. So you must want somebody else. **(6)** _____

Suspect Word #2: You think you're so smart? Okay, if I'm a crime, then which one am I? I could be a number of very serious offenses. It's not me.
(7) _____

Suspect Word #3: I'm not a crime, although I may feel like one to some people. I'm simply an insult, a slap in the face. **(8)** _____

Which one did Betty think was the serious crime? Explain why you chose that suspect.
_____
_____

GOING BEYOND

Use each of the words on the list in a sentence. Make a story out of your sentences.

Emily Taproot

Name _____ Date _____

I think that I shall never see

A poem lovely as a tree.

—Joyce Kilmer

Emily Taproot's Poetry Workshop

Welcome to Poetry Workshop. I'm Emily Taproot, a board-certified, licensed poet with a Master's Degree in Rhythm, Rhyme, and Clever Wordplay. Today, we will work with Joyce Kilmer's well-known verse. By changing different words, we can change the meaning of the poem.

Complete each verse of the poem below using words from the Word List. Use the definitions in the box to help you.

Word List

chum: friend
composed: made of
conviction: strongly held belief
devoid: totally lacking
dignified: worthy of respect
discern: to see or recognize
engage: to become involved with
entity: a thing
eschew: to avoid
indifferent: not caring what happens

microscopic: so small that it can only be seen under magnification
mobile: able to move
rumor: unpleasant and often untrue story that is passed on
stout: bold, strong, and thick
surmise: to make a guess
taciturn: not talkative
ultimately: in the end
virtues: good and notable traits

1. I think that I shall never see
   An **(a)** _____
   as **(b)** _____ as a tree.

2. Though stately and quite **(c)** _____
   Trees often lack a **(d)** _____ side.

(a) a thing that exists
(b) unconcerned, uninterested
(c) noble
(d) capable of moving

36

Name _____ Date _____

Emily Taproot

3. Here's one thing that I cannot **(e)** _____:
   Just why are trees so **(f)** _____?

4. Trees are painfully shy—that's the **(g)** _____
   And totally **(h)** _____ of a sense of humor.

5. **(i)** _____ a tree on any topic
   Their level of interest is **(j)** _____!

6. I **(k)** _____ that trees are incapable of seeing
   The **(l)** _____ of a human being.

7. It is my **(m)** _____ that in the end
   A tree just cannot be your friend.

8. Trees are tall, strong, **(n)** _____, and good
   But **(o)** _____, they're
   (p) _____ of wood!

9. So if you seek a loyal **(q)** _____
   (r) _____ the tree—they're just no fun!

(e) recognize
(f) quiet; without words

(g) story that is spread
(h) without

(i) to become involved with
(j) very small

(k) to guess
(l) good qualities

(m) strongly held belief

(n) thick and strong

(o) lastly
(p) made of

(q) small amount
(r) keep away from

GOING BEYOND
Write three rhyming couplets about your favorite plant. Include words from the Word List in your poem.

Eddie Snively: World's Biggest Liar

"HELLO, I'M PENNY KNUCKLES. TODAY I'LL BE INTERVIEWING EDDIE SNIVELY, WHO WAS RECENTLY CROWNED "LIAR OF THE YEAR" AT THE LIARS' INTERNATIONAL ASSOCIATION RALLY (L.I.A.R.) IN LAS VEGAS."

Write a word from the Word List below to complete each sentence in the interview.

Word List

- **allege**: claim to be true
- **appellation**: name
- **assert**: to state clearly
- **categorically**: absolutely
- **characterize**: to describe
- **commend**: to praise
- **conceive**: to understand
- **convocation**: a meeting
- **coronation**: crowning
- **decorative**: for purposes of decoration
- **duplicity**: trickery; untruth
- **embossed**: carved or stamped
- **galaxy**: a large group of stars
- **incidentally**: by the way
- **outrage**: a disgraceful act
- **prevaricating**: lying
- **refute**: to deny
- **relentless**: unstopping
- **triumph**: victory
- **unaware**: not knowing about

Penny: First of all, I'd like to **(1)** _____ you on winning your award. You did a wonderful job! How does it feel to be Liar of the Year?

Eddie: I cannot **(2)** _____ of what you're talking about. What award?

Penny: Why, the Liar of the Year award. Your **(3)** _____ was just this afternoon. Right here in Las Vegas.

Eddie: Hey, what **(4)** _____ are you from? Did your spaceship just land? I didn't get any award today. I was home. In bed. Yeah, that's where I was, in bed.

Penny: Do you mean to **(5)** _____ the idea that you won the Liar of the Year Award right here in front of 50,000 people?

Eddie: I **(6)** _____ reject the idea. There is no way I attended the L.I.A.R. convention!

Name _____ **Date** _____

Eddie Snively

Penny: But there were witnesses to your **(7)** _____. Fifty thousand people saw you hold the trophy over your head. Could they all be wrong?

Eddie: Sure. It was a liars' **(8)** _____, wasn't it? So it's obvious: they were all liars.

Penny: How can I be sure that you're not **(9)** _____ right now yourself?

Eddie: Because I'm not a liar. Do you **(10)** _____ that I am?

Penny: Well, let me put it this way: why do I see a trophy **(11)** _____ with the words EDDIE SNIVELY: LIAR OF THE YEAR on it? And here is a photograph of you accepting the trophy.

Eddie: What trophy? What photo? I'm **(12)** _____ of what you are talking about.

Penny: This trophy right here! And this photograph! How else would you **(13)** _____ these two things?

Eddie: I'd call this so-called trophy a paperweight. And this thing over here is not a photograph of me. I have never worn my hair like that. And **(14)** _____, I've never laid eyes on either one of these things before in my life.

Penny: Now let me get this straight. In this photo, you **(15)** _____ that this is not you, Eddie Snively, receiving the trophy.

Eddie: Who's Eddie Snively? Who said my **(16)** _____ was Eddie Snively?

Penny: Then who are you? This **(17)** _____ award says EDDIE SNIVELY in beautiful script on it, doesn't it?

Eddie: Well, who says this is my award? How do we know that someone isn't engaging in a bit of **(18)** _____ by planting this here?

Penny: I can see how you won this award. You're completely **(19)** _____. You never tell the truth, do you?

Eddie: Who, me? Are you calling me a liar? This is an **(20)** _____! I've never been so insulted in my entire life. This interview is over!

GOING BEYOND

Write an interview between Penny and the winner of the WORLD'S MOST HONEST PERSON award. Use as many words as you can from the Word List.

Bingo Hackles, Sports Reporter

My name is Bingo Hackles. I'm a sports reporter for the Daily Sports Fiend. Recently, my boss at the Fiend told me that my articles needed more **IMPORTANT-SOUNDING WORDS** in them. Well, I need help!

Please help me edit this poem about a basketball game between the Mudville Mudhens and the Bay City Red Birds.

Replace each boldfaced word with a word from the Word List below.

Word List

- **ascended:** went up
- **braced:** readied oneself for an event
- **carom:** a bounce off at an angle
- **wavered:** hesitated
- **descended:** went down
- **eliminated:** got rid of
- **fleet:** fast on his or her feet
- **fortunately:** with luck
- **initiated:** started
- **locale:** a place or location
- **plucked:** pulled off abruptly
- **proficiency:** competence
- **propelled:** pushed forward
- **radiates:** sends out rays
- **reckoning:** act of counting
- **resumed:** to start over
- **thunderstruck:** astonished
- **transferred:** sent from one person to another
- **undoubtedly:** without any dispute
- **unquestionably:** beyond questioning

Name _____ Date _____

Bingo Hackles

1. The **score** stood 44 to 43 against the Mudville Five that day. _____
2. Fouls **knocked out** Parker so Coach put Tracy in to play. _____
3. Now Tracy wasn't **swift** and she also wasn't tall. _____
4. In fact, she had little, if any, playing **skill** at all. _____
5. So when the game **started again**, we had our fingers crossed. _____
6. But out there on the court, Tracy seemed **completely** lost. _____
7. Suddenly the Red Birds missed, and the **rebound** came to Miles. _____
8. She **grabbed** it off the rim as the Mudville fans went wild. _____
9. Then **passed** it up to Barkney who was running toward the stands. _____
10. Barkney flipped the ball to Austin, but it **dropped** in Tracy's hands. _____
11. Now Tracy tried to shoot but she **launched** a feeble missile. _____
12. **Luckily** for Tracy came the tweet of the referee's whistle. _____
13. "Two foul shots!" barked the ref, as the fans **waited** for the worst. _____
14. And Tracy, looking **surprised**, went and promptly missed the first. _____
15. A quiet Tracy **paused** with two seconds on the clock. _____
16. And **shot** the final free throw as the stands began to rock. _____
17. And as the ball **arose** the gym got deadly quiet. _____
18. If Tracy missed the shot, there would **surely** be a riot. _____
19. Oh, somewhere the sun **shines**, life is good; good guys win. _____
20. But that **somewhere** isn't Mudville, because Tracy's shot _____

   ... did NOT

   ... go in!

GOING BEYOND

Choose five words from the Word List and list their synonyms. You may use a thesaurus or dictionary to help you.

The Four Vocabularians

Fighting Crime With Nothing But Words!

BONGO · NINA · MURPH · PINKY

Today's Episode: Dr. Dialect's Dictionary of Deception

The sun shone brightly over Rochelle Park, home of the Four Vocabularians. At the clubhouse, Murph **burnished** his Quizmo game board with lemon oil and a rag while Nina solved crossword puzzles. Pinky read her thesaurus while Bongo **composed** original songs on the Vocab-O-Computer.

Suddenly, Dr. Dialect's **repulsive** face **materialized** on the Vocab-O-Computer screen. Bongo covered his eyes in horror. He peeked through his fingers and read:

GREETINGS 4 VOCABULARIANS! I HOPE YOU ARE HAVING A FINE DAY, BECAUSE IF YOU DON'T GIVE ME $1 BILLION I WILL **OBLITERATE** TEN WORDS IN THE ENGLISH LANGUAGE FOREVER!

"Look at this!" called Bongo. The Four Vocabularians gathered around the Vocab-O-Computer screen.

"Do away with a ten words?" Murph cried. "How can he do that?"

"Easy," Dr. Dialect's voice on the screen said. "I'll just list the words in my Dr. Dialect's Dictionary of **Deception**."

"Dictionary of Deception?" Pinky asked. "How can a dictionary trick people?"

"It's a **confounding** dictionary in which all of the definitions are wrong," Dr. Dialect said. "The idea is—if people use words sloppily and incorrectly the words eventually lose their meaning."

"What an **ingenious** plan," Bongo said. "This may be your best idea yet. Too bad you'll never get away with it, Dr. Dialect."

"You don't think so?" Dr. Dialect said. He **cackled** with a laugh that made Nina cover her ears. "Well, take a look at t-t-thisss-s-s!"

And with that, Dr. Dialect's face faded from the screen, leaving the list of the 16 **endangered** words with their incorrect definitions.

Murph said, "These are great words. We can't afford to let them lose their meaning."

"What do we do?" asked Pinky.

"VOCABULARIANS—to ACTION!" cried Nina, raising her arm.

Four Vocabularians

Name _____ Date _____

Take time out from the story to write the letter of the correct definition next to each word. To find your answers, use the context clues given in the story

____ 1. burnished	A. put at risk
____ 2. cackled	B. laughed shrilly
____ 3. composed	C. confusing
____ 4. deception	D. appeared suddenly
____ 5. endangered	E. wrote or created something, especially music or poetry
____ 6. ingenious	F. misleading; false trickery
____ 7. materialized	G. brilliant, clever, smartly done
____ 8. obliterate	H. ugliness that drives one away
____ 9. confounding	I. destroyed completely
____ 10. repulsive	J. made smooth by polishing

One Hour Later

Dr. Dialect appeared on the screen. "Well, Vocabularians," he said, "looks like I've outsmarted you this time." Then he gaped at the words on the screen in horror. "No!" he cried. "It can't be!"

"It is!" said Pinky. "We CHANGED all of your wrong definitions, Dialect! Instead of the wrong definitions, your words now have the correct definitions."

"No no, N-N-N-N-N-NO-O-O-O-O-OOOOO!" cried Dr. Dialect, as his face slowly faded away on the screen.

"Well, I guess that takes care of that," said Murph. "How about a game of Quizmo, fellow Vocabularians?"

"Good idea," said Nina. "Right after we finish this crossword puzzle together."

"What about playing a thesaurus game?" asked Pinky.

"Right," said Bongo, "as soon as we finish singing this song I just wrote."

They all laughed.

"Gee," said Bongo, "I guess there's only one thing we all agree on: when you play fast and loose with words—they start to lose their meaning."

"You can say that again," said Murph.

GOING BEYOND

Dr. Dialect's next deed is to remove endings from words. Help Dr. D by choosing four words from the Word List and writing them without their word endings.

43

Name _____   Date _____

Laverne Weaselford, U.S. Senator

Senator Weaselford likes to write her own speeches rather than employ a speechwriter. But the senator's vocabulary is weak.

Fill in the missing vocabulary of her speech using the words in the Word List.

Word List

- **amend:** to make a formal, legal change
- **candidate:** person running for elected office
- **critical:** very important; crucial, decisive
- **defame:** to damage someone's name
- **federal:** relating to the national government
- **incarceration:** a stay in jail
- **nominate:** to name a person to run for office
- **prohibiting:** forbidding or preventing
- **reform:** to improve or correct social or economic conditions
- **righteous:** fair and just
- **statute:** law made by an elected body
- **submit:** to offer for consideration
- **violators:** those who break a law

My fellow Americans, my name is Laverne Weaselford. I am the U.S. Senator from this (1) _____ state that has always treated a Weaselford fairly. I stand before you tonight to present bills that I plan to (2) _____ on your behalf to the Senate. These bills address the most (3) _____ issues that face our country today: family and election reform.

The first bill is the Weaselford Family Protection Bill. It would make it a (4) _____ crime for anyone in any way to harm a Weaselford. For it would be a national issue to even tease a Weaselford or (5) _____ a Weaselford by calling any one of us "Weasel," "Goofball," or "Smeaselford." (6) _____ who break this law would be subject to (7) _____ in prison for 50 years.

I would also like to (8) _____ the Weaselford Election Reform Bill to have a new focus. This bill would clean up the election process by (9) _____ citizens from voting for (10) _____ who are born with last names other than Weaselford. If the people running for office are named "Jones" or "Waistband," you can't vote for them.

I expect your full support on these issues, or my name isn't Queen Weaselford—I mean, Senator Weaselford!

GOING BEYOND

Make up a political speech about the laws you are introducing to Congress. Use at least five of the words from the Vocabulary List above.

Marla Murgatroid, Romance Novelist

IT'S HARD TO BELIEVE, BUT EVEN I, MARLA MURGATROID, THE WORLD'S GREATEST ROMANCE NOVELIST, SOMETIMES MAKES MISTAKES. MY EDITOR, EDWINA "ED" TEDSON, SENT ME A LIST OF CORRECTIONS FOR THE MANUSCRIPT OF MY LATEST BOOK, UTTERLY TOTALLY ABSOLUTELY. PERHAPS YOU CAN HELP ME.

Replace each boldfaced word with a word from the Word List below. Use the editor's clues provided by Edwina "Ed" Tedson.

Word List

- **cherish:** hold dear
- **dearest:** someone who is greatly loved
- **gorgeous:** very beautiful
- **lithe:** strong, flexible, graceful
- **lounged:** lay comfortably
- **lustrous:** shiny and beautiful
- **marvelous:** remarkable
- **pounding:** striking repeatedly with great force
- **prevailing:** winning
- **radiant:** giving off light
- **sonorous:** deep and pleasant in sound
- **stammered:** stuttered
- **sultry:** humid, sweltering, lush
- **throb:** to beat rapidly
- **unmistakable:** obvious

1. It was a hot and **gooey** day at the beach club. _____
   Ed: Change "gooey" into something hot and lush.

2. Dominique D'Amour **slumped** by the water's edge. _____
   Ed: Not "slumped." Something more relaxed.

3. Her raven-colored hair gave off a **foggy** sheen in the bright sunlight. _____
   Ed: "Foggy" hair is crummy. Make her hair healthy and beautiful.

4. Dominique was **okay-looking** beyond all compare. _____
   Ed: She's more than just "okay-looking." Come on!

Name _____ Date _____

Marla Murgatroid

5. On a nearby tennis court, Hoover LeDue was **grunting** in a match against Skippy Barksdale. _____
    Ed: Instead of "grunting," have LeDue ahead in the match.

6. "**Lucky** shot, LeDue!" shouted Skippy Barksdale. _____
    Ed: Have Skippy compliment LeDue on a great shot.

7. Suddenly, the image of Dominique flashed through LeDue's mind. "She needs me," LeDue uttered in his **whiny** voice. _____
    Ed: Give LeDue a deep rather than a "whiny" voice.

8. Taking long, **bumbling** strides, LeDue raced over to the beach. _____
    Ed: Not "bumbling;" flexible and graceful.

9. Dominique's **crooked** face was nowhere to be seen. _____
    Ed: Dominique's face should seem to give off light.

10. Had she vanished in the **snoring** surf? _____
    Ed: Surf doesn't "snore." Make it come in hard and fast.

11. LeDue's heart suddenly began to **yodel** in his chest. _____
    Ed: Why would his heart "yodel"? A heart beats.

12. Suddenly, LeDue heard Dominique's **tedious** voice. _____
    Ed: It's a voice that he would never fail to recognize.

13. "Over here, **buster**," Dominique cooed, walking towards the beach with two lemonades. _____
    Ed: Call him something more loving than "buster."

14. "D-Dominique!" he **barked**. "Y-you're still here!" _____
    Ed: He's not a dog. He's having trouble getting his words out.

15. "I'll always **ignore** you, as long as I live," Hoover LeDue said. _____
    Ed: He doesn't want to ignore her. He wants to love her! Remember, you are writing a romance novel!

GOING BEYOND

What will happen next? Will Dominique and Hoover's romance survive? Write a paragraph telling what will happen next in the story. Use as many of the words from the Word List as you can.

46

Emily Taproot, Vocabulary Poet: The Language of Love

This is Emily Taproot, poet of the heart. Today I am going to share my new poem with you, "How Do I Love Thee." It is actually based on an old poem, but I have changed the words.

Word List

aloft: high in the air
contorting: twisting, wrenching, or bending out of place
debase: to lower in quality
discretion: carefulness, responsible
efface: to erase
embrace: to hold or hug
expeditiously: with speed and efficiency
flawless: perfect, without defects
flitting: darting nimbly and rapidly
fragrance: pleasant aroma

grizzled: old, streaked with gray
hurtling: moving with great speed
inconspicuous: not obvious; hidden
interface: surface at which contact takes place
ludicrous: ridiculous
phase: a distinct stage in a series
persistently: not stopping
relinquish: to give up
tenacious: the quality of holding on tightly
pungent: sharp, biting smell or taste

Complete the poem with words from the Word List. Hint: Every line rhymes.

How Do I Love Thee
How do I love thee? Let me count the ways:

1. My love is like the moon above, no matter what its _____.
2. My love is like a ballerina, _____ with style and grace.

Name _____ Date _____

3. My love is a monarch butterfly, _____ from place to place.

4. My love is a teacher's pet, _____ seeking praise.

5. My love is a delightful _____, whose odor lingers for days.

6. My love is written in indelible ink, impossible to _____.

7. My love is as old as a _____ fisherman, fishing for manta rays.

8. My love is a speedy racehorse, _____ winning every race.

9. My love is a newborn pup, smothered in it's mother's _____.

10. My love uses the utmost _____, never proceeding in haste.

11. My love is a _____ barnacle, impossible to displace.

12. My love can be _____, hiding in another place.

13. My love is a piece of chewing gum, with a _____ peppermint taste.

14. My love is like a computer, with a high-tech _____.

15. My love is a high-flying astronaut, _____ through outer space.

16. My love is ever the hunter, it will never _____ the chase.

17. My love is the highest quality, impossible to _____.

18. My love can seem quite _____, but it never ceases to amaze.

19. My love's a professional wrestler, _____ your neck out of place.

20. My love is ever the poet, in search of the _____ phrase.

GOING BEYOND

Use words from the Word List to help Emily complete the following poem.
How Does My Hair Flow?
How does my hair flow? Let me count the ways:
My hair is . . .

The Four Vocabularians

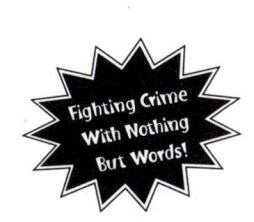

Fighting Crime With Nothing But Words!

BONGO   NINA   MURPH   PINKY

Today's Episode: The National Word Day Speech

It wasn't just any day in Rochelle Park. It was National Word Day, and the Four Vocabularians were gathered around the TV in their clubhouse, awaiting the annual speech from the President of the United States.

"My fellow . . ." the president began. "Wha—uh—uh. Um."

"What's going on?" asked Murph, as the president continued to stutter and mumble. Suddenly an evil face appeared on the screen.

Dr. Dialect!

"Hello, America," the evil genius crowed. "I, Dr. Dialect, have STOLEN the President's speech! I replaced key words in the speech with slang expressions."

"The president sounds like a fool!" Pinky cried.

"We've got to do something," said Nina. "Bongo, get on the Vocab-O-Computer and see if you can get a transcript of the president's speech."

"I think I've got it," said Bongo, fiddling with computer keys.

Take time out from the story to replace each slang expression from the president's speech with one of the words from the Word List.

Word List

budget: an organized plan for money
citizens: people who live in a place
conclude: to come to an end or close
entreat: to make a strong request; beg

festivities: joyous celebration
generate: to bring into being
grave: extremely serious
illegitimate: not legal
inessential: not necessary

jeopardy: state of danger, risk, or peril
penalize: to punish for breaking a rule
pledge: a promise
predicament: a troublesome situation
redundant: a repetition of what you already have
regret: to feel sorry that something occurs
revenue: incoming money
salvage: to save
sufficient: enough

Four Vocabularians

Name _____   Date _____

TRANSCRIPT OF THE PRESIDENT'S SPEECH ON NATIONAL WORD DAY

1. My fellow American *dudes and dudettes*, I stand before you today to speak about our nation's *like, you know, money and stuff*. _____ _____

2. The *green stuff* we collected for National Word Day is not *A-okay* for our needs. _____ _____

3. This puts our nation into a *like, totally serious bad scene*. _____ _____

4. I *feel completely bummed out* to announce that National Word Day is now in like *trouble-city, if you know what I mean*. _____ _____

5. Each year, Americans use millions of unneeded type words in a variety of *totally bogus* ways. _____ _____

6. I hereby make a *double-pinkie promise* to *like totally save* our celebration using what I call the National Unnecessary Word Tax, or NUWT. _____ _____

7. The NUWT tax will *turn the screws on words* that are unnecessary or *like, reruns of themselves*. _____ _____

8. This tax should be able to *whip up* billions of dollars for our National Word Day *wing-ding*. _____ _____

9. Before I *bug out*, ladies and gentlemen, *I am on my hands and knees for you* to support NUWT. Thank you and good night. _____ _____

15 MINUTES LATER...

"The president's speech is ruined!" bragged Dr. Dialect. "He sounds like a fool. Your precious National Word Day is ruined, Vocabularians!"

"Not so fast, Dialect," said Bongo. "Take a look at this!" With several swift keystrokes Bongo emailed Dr. Dialect the CORRECTED copy of the president's speech.

"What's this?" Dr. Dialect cried. "Oh no! It can't be! I'm ruined. Ruined! RUINED!" With that Dr. Dialect faded from the screen.

"Well, what now?" Bongo asked

"Let's have an old-fashioned National Word Day celebration!" Pinky cried.

So that's what they did. And everyone had a great time!

GOING BEYOND

You have been selected to be the fifth Vocabularian. Find synonyms for five words in the Word List. Record them for the Vocabularians to use in the future.

Name _____   Date _____

WELCOME TO THE 58TH ANNUAL NATIONAL WORD AWARDS...

The Wordies

Weeza: I'm your host, Weeza Dangles.

Dirk: And I'm your cohost, Dirk Zero. Hey, it's been a great year for words, Weeza. Did you know that something like eight hundred million ka-jillion words were spoken, written, whispered, or uttered last year?

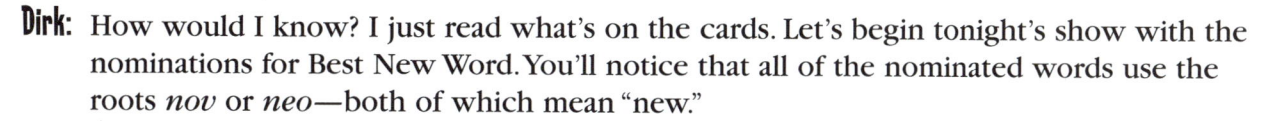

Weeza: Wow, that's a lot of blabbing, Dirk. Is that really true?

Dirk: How would I know? I just read what's on the cards. Let's begin tonight's show with the nominations for Best New Word. You'll notice that all of the nominated words use the roots *nov* or *neo*—both of which mean "new."

Weeza: Hey, that's "news" to me, Dirk! [audience explodes with laughter]. Why don't you go ahead and sing us your nomination song?

Dirk: Use the clues in my song to define each boldface nominated word. [launches into a musical song]:

♪ I'M A **NEOPHYTE** SINGER. I'M A **NEOPHYTE** DANCER. ♪
♪ IF YOU THINK I AM EXPERIENCED, YOU DO NOT HAVE THE ANSWER. ♪
MY ACT IS NOT A **NOVELTY**, BUT IT'S FULL OF **INNOVATION**.
♪ I THINK IT CAN BE FIXED WITH JUST A TOUCH OF **RENOVATION**. ♪

Match each word to its definition.

Best "New" Word

1.	neophyte	A.	new and unusual thing
2.	neologism	B.	new way of doing something
3.	novelty	C.	beginner
4.	innovation	D.	make new by fixing
5.	renovation	E.	new word

Dirk: [opens the envelope]: ...And the Wordie goes to *neologism*. Accepting on behalf of *neologism* is myself, Mr. Dirk Zero. [thunderous applause]

Dirk: Thank you very much. Thank you. Thank you. I just can't describe how great I feel right now. I wish there were a word for it...

Weeza: And now, to present the awards for Best Comedy Word, superstar comedienne Suzy Chuckles. [Suzy walks across the stage.]

Suzy: Hi, I'm superstar comedienne Suzy Chuckles. I'm so goofy and funny that I crack myself up. That's why I'm here to present the nominees for Best Comedy Word.

The Wordies

Name _____ Date _____

Write a definition for each Comedy Word. Use context clues to help you.

Best Comedy Word

6. I really try to crack people up with my **facetious** remarks. And I'm not being **facetious** when I say this. **Facetious** means _____

7. I use **irony** to say the opposite of what I mean. Or mean the opposite of what I say. In any event, this tends to crack people up. **Irony** means _____

8. Sometimes I use **sarcasm** to make fun of people in a mean way. I feel bad about this, but it still cracks people up. **Sarcasm** means _____

9. I'm so darn funny that I can even crack people up making faces and burping noises. It may be silly or **asinine** but I do it anyway. **Asinine** means _____

10. I'm known for **whimsical** jokes that are light-hearted and gentle. Do these jokes crack people up? What do you think? **Whimsical** means _____

Suzy [opens the envelope]: And the Wordie goes to *asinine*. [titanic applause] Accepting on behalf of *asinine* is me, Ms. Suzy Chuckles. Thank you Suzy, thank you very much. You know, I'd like to say that this is really an asinine award. Thank you very much.

Weeza: And now, the moment we've all been waiting for—The Word of the Year. I'll sing this nomination song myself. You'll notice that each boldfaced word has the root *ann* or *enn*, which means "year."

♪ HAPPY **ANNIVERSARY** (ONCE AGAIN) — IT'S MY **ANNUAL** COMPLAINT. ♪
♪ ANOTHER YEAR WITHOUT AN AWARD, I'M SO DESPERATE I COULD FAINT ♪
BEFORE I BECOME **SUPERANNUATED**, I'D LIKE TO WIN ONE WORDIE
♪ I'VE FACE **PERENNIAL** DISAPPOINTMENT, EVERY YEAR SINCE I WAS THIRTY! ♪

Weeza: And the Wordie goes to *perennial*. Oh, I'm so happy! How can I ever thank you? I'll be *perennially* grateful. I really will.

Dirk: Goodnight, everyone!

[Applause. Applause. Applause.]

Match each word to its definition.

Word of The "Year"

11. anniversary	A. old in years
12. perennial	B. yearly celebration
13. superannuated	C. yearly
14. annual	D. every year forever

GOING BEYOND
Use the three "award-winning" words in a short paragraph.

Name _____ Date _____

Buck Bickley's Big Braggin' Book

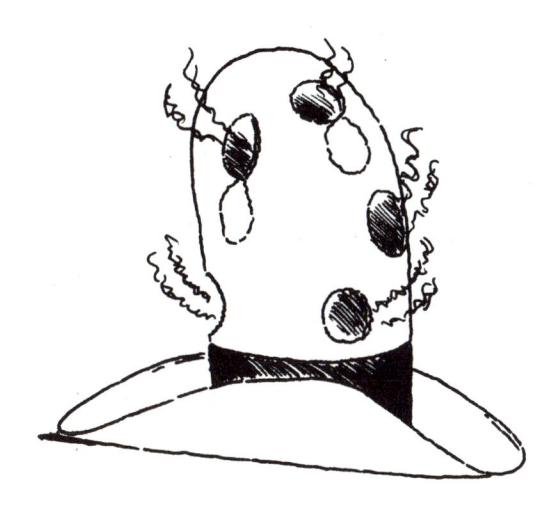

HOWDY, I'M BUCK BICKLEY. WELCOME TO MY BIG BRAGGIN' BOOK. IF YOU LIKE BRAGGIN', THIS IS THE PLACE TO COME. IN THIS BOOK YOU'LL HEAR ME BRAGGIN' ABOUT
- ★ HOW DOGGONE SMART I AM
- ★ WHAT A DOGGONE GREAT GUY I AM
- ★ HOW MUCH DOGGONE STUFF I HAVE
- ★ HOW DOGGONE SMART MY DOGGONE DOG IS

SO PULL UP A CHAIR AND SETTLE DOWN TO SOME GOOD OLD FASHIONED BRAGGIN', THE BUCK BICKLEY WAY.

Word List

affluent: wealthy
candid: frank, honest
denomination: name of a group of things with a particular value
disperse: scatter
distinct: clear, easily recalled
droll: amusing in a strange way
elite: members of the finest group
expansive: grand in size and scale

keen: sharp and quick with the five senses
modest: humble, not boastful
penetrating: passing through by piercing
perilous: dangerous
polyglot: speaking many languages
resplendently: in a dazzling, brightly shining way
violation: a breaking of a law or rule

Buck left some words out of his book. Complete the sentences with words from the Word List above.

1. I'm so smart they're thinkin' of puttin' my face on the twenty-dollar bill. Except with me on it, the _____ would go up to twenty-one dollars!

2. My dog is so smart he's got a diploma from Harvard, Yale, and other _____ universities even though he never graduated from high school. He only finished grades K-9. (Get it: canine?)

53

Name _____ **Date** _____

Buck Bickley

3. I'm so good-looking that it's sometimes _____ for me to go out in public. That's why on the street outside my house there's a sign that says DANGER: HANDSOME MAN ZONE.

4. I'm so _____ that I never toot my own horn. In fact, when I drive my car, the horn toots itself!

5. I'm so _____ brilliant that light bulbs often look dull next to me.

6. My memory is so _____ that I often remember things that haven't even occurred yet.

7. My eyesight is so _____ that I can often see things that aren't even there.

8. My _____ dog is so smart that he barks in three different languages.

9. Some of my thoughts are so _____ that I often get holes in my hat.

10. I'm so _____ that when I play Monopoly I use real money.

11. My house is so _____ that I need to hail a cab to get from the kitchen to the bedroom.

12. I'm such a talented gardener that I can _____ toothpicks in the soil in the spring that will come up as fence posts in the fall.

13. I'm so _____ that even when I try to fib it comes out truthful.

14. My jokes are so _____ that people laugh at them even when they're not funny.

15. My car is so fast that I once received a speeding _____ when it was still parked.

GOING BEYOND
Can you outbrag Buck Bickley? Write three brags using as many words from the Word Box as you can.

Buck Bickley's Dog's Big Braggin' Book

I'M BUCK BICKLEY'S DOG "FLASH." IF YOU LIKE BOOKS WHERE DOGS DO A LOT OF BRAGGIN', THEN THIS IS THE BIG, BRAGGIN' BOOK FOR YOU. IN THIS BOOK I'LL BE BRAGGIN' ABOUT:
- ★ HOW DOGGONE CLEVER I AM
- ★ WHAT A DOGGONE GREAT DOG I AM
- ★ HOW MUCH DOGGONE GREAT STUFF I HAVE

SO LET THE BRAGGIN' BEGIN!

Word List

- **amiable:** friendly
- **compassionate:** deep feelings for others
- **frequently:** happening very often
- **ideal:** a model of excellence
- **peerless:** without equal; the best
- **prosperous:** successful
- **pursue:** to follow
- **retrieve:** to get back
- **secluded:** in a remote, hidden place
- **shrewd:** sly

Write a word from the list to replace each underlined word.

1. For a dog, I'm rich. How <u>well-off</u> am I? When it's time to <u>fetch</u> the newspaper, I hire someone else to do it. _____ _____

2. For a dog, I'm a fast runner. In fact, when I <u>chase</u> my tail I <u>often</u> catch up with it. I often even pass it by. This, I find, is a good way of making ends meet. _____ _____

3. I'm so <u>smart</u>, I've been known to outfox a fox. And I'm much wiser and <u>caring</u> than your average owl. Despite their reputations, I find that most owls really don't give a hoot. _____ _____

4. I'm so <u>popular</u> that cats even like me. My luxurious 40-room doghouse is so <u>private</u> that it doesn't have pests like ants—they can't find out where it is! _____ _____

5. Hey, what can I say? I'm a <u>special</u> dog. In the dictionary under the word "extraordinary" it shows a picture of me! You know I'm the <u>perfect</u> pet. Just ask Buck Bickley, because he never stretches the truth. _____ _____

GOING BEYOND

Have you heard Buck Bickley's hamster? She can outbrag both Buck and the dog! Write a dialogue between Buck, his dog, and his hamster. Use at least five words from the Word List.

Name _____ Date _____

Julie Kablooie's Hollywood Gossip Column

IT'S JULIE KABLOOIE— YOUR NUMBER ONE HOLLYWOOD SNOOP WITH THE INSIDE SCOOP, THE DUCHESS OF DISH, THE REGENT OF RUMOR, THE CZARINA OF CHATTER, AND THE SUPERINTENDENT OF THE SKINNY.

Circle the correct synonym for each boldfaced word.

ITEM 1: PEACHES LOSES IT ON THE SET!

Peaches Mung, popular child star of "Peaches," "Hi, I'm Peaches," and "Peaches Is Back!", reportedly blew her cool on the set of the new movie, "Hi, I'm Peaches II." Peaches **harangued** the cast in a 45-minute speech about being "serious" on the set, after which she vanished for two hours for an "important ice cream break." The cast, which includes heartthrob Dirk Delbart, was **livid**. But Peaches wasn't **fazed**. She told Director Boz Boggly that if he tried to **reprove** her in any way she would walk off the movie, "and then what would they title it?"

1. **harangued** (a) ranted (b) exercised (c) snoozed (d) sang
2. **livid** (a) alive (b) not alive (c) very angry (d) happy
3. **fazed** (a) late (b) troubled (c) heavy (d) alone
4. **reprove** (a) hug (b) scold (c) smell (d) improve

ITEM 2: WILL BOZ AND BETTI TIE THE KNOT?

Betti Fetching is a Hollywood legend. Betti's **extraordinary** career has had more blockbuster hits than most stars have toes on their feet. Betti is an actor's actor, a star among stars, a **luminary** among the lesser lights. So what is she doing with Director Boz Boggly? I mean, really! Boz is a good director and everything (currently filming "Hi, I'm Peaches II," with Peaches Mung). But that **scraggly** beard? Come on, Boz, either shave it or grow it! Those rumpled **dungarees**? No one has worn that look since the 20th Century! Get a new stylist, would you, Boz? Then you can come back and talk marriage with our beloved Betti.

5. **extraordinary** (a) average (b) too much (c) remarkable (d) typical
6. **luminary** (a) beginner (b) failure (c) bright light (d) square
7. **scraggly** (a) flowing (b) long (c) messy (d) shaved
8. **dungarees** (a) jeans (b) shoes (c) words (d) noodles

GOING BEYOND
Select four vocabulary words. Write an antonym (a word with the opposite meaning) for each.

Freelance Know-It All

Name _____ Date _____

Do You Have What It Takes to Become a Freelance Know-It-All Reviewer?

HAVE YOU EVER SEEN A MOVIE OR BOOK REVIEW AND THOUGHT TO YOURSELF, "I COULD WRITE A BETTER REVIEW THAN THAT"? WELL, HERE'S YOUR CHANCE. TRY WRITING REVIEWS OF THE BOOK *THE BIG HICCUP* BY VICTOR KNEEPORT. FIRST WRITE A POSITIVE REVIEW OF THE BOOK. THEN WRITE ANOTHER REVIEW OF THE SAME BOOK, ONLY THIS TIME MAKE IT A NEGATIVE REVIEW.

Use words from the word list to complete a positive review. Then use different words to complete a negative review.

Word List for The Big Hiccup

- **abject:** low and miserable
- **banal:** commonplace and predictable
- **clichés:** overused expressions
- **detested:** disliked intensely
- **edified:** instructed in a positive way
- **extraordinary:** excellent; beyond normal
- **fiasco:** complete failure
- **insipid:** dull
- **inspired:** stimulated and aroused
- **lucid:** totally clear
- **profound:** deep and meaningful
- **relished:** keenly enjoyed
- **shoddy:** sloppy
- **trite:** unoriginal, flat, weak
- **triumph:** a victory
- **unqualified:** absolute
- **witticisms:** clever remarks

THE BIG HICCUP, A BOOK BY VICTOR KNEEPOT

A Positive Review by _____ (your name here)

This book was an **(1)** _____ **(2)** _____. The premise was **(3)** _____—a young boy gets himself in trouble when he gets the hiccups at the wrong time. How **(4)** _____! The writing style was **(5)** _____ and full of **(6)** _____. I found myself to be truly **(7)** _____ by the book. To summarize, I **(8)** _____ every word of this **(9)** _____ book.

THE BIG HICCUP, A BOOK BY VICTOR KNEEPOT

A Negative Review by _____ (your name here)

This book was an **(10)** _____ **(11)** _____. The premise

57

Name _____ **Date** _____

Freelance Know-It All

was **(12)** _____—a young boy gets himself in trouble when he gets the hiccups at the wrong time. How **(13)** _____! The writing style was **(14)** _____ and full of **(15)** _____. To summarize, I **(16)** _____ every word of this **(17)** _____ book.

Word List for My Little Sister, The Train

- **bungling:** clumsy
- **convincing:** able to persuade
- **excels:** does something with great skill
- **exceptional:** better than all others
- **falters:** is unsteady
- **farfetched:** not believable
- **fascinating:** very interesting
- **intrigue:** to fascinate
- **mediocre:** ordinary or worse
- **poignant:** moving, touching, meaningful
- **pointless:** without purpose
- **tedium:** something that is boring
- **vacuous:** empty
- **winsome:** charming

MY LITTLE SISTER, THE TRAIN: A FILM STARRING BONNIE BILGE AND CINDY SNARKUS

<u>A Positive Review</u> by _____

The movie begins with a **(18)** _____ premise: what if your seven-year-old sister were transformed into a 200-ton locomotive? The **(19)** _____ begins as Cindy the Train tries to do ordinary things, like go to school and eat an ice cream cone. Bonnie Bilge is **(20)** _____ as the older sister. Cindy Snarkus **(21)** _____ as the **(22)** _____ seven-year-old who is turned into a train. I couldn't help but cry during the many **(23)** _____ moments in this **(24)** _____ film.

MY LITTLE SISTER, THE TRAIN: A FILM STARRING BONNIE BILGE AND CINDY SNARKUS

<u>A Negative Review</u> by _____

The movie begins with a **(25)** _____ premise: what if your seven-year-old sister were transformed into a 200-ton locomotive? The **(26)** _____ begins as Cindy the Train tries to do ordinary things, like go to school and eat an ice cream cone. Bonnie Bilge is **(27)** _____ as the older sister. Cindy Snarkus **(28)** _____ as the **(29)** _____ seven-year-old who is turned into a train. I couldn't help but cry during the many **(30)** _____ moments in this **(31)** _____ film.

GOING BEYOND

Think about the last movie you saw. Would you give it a positive or a negative review? Write a short review of the movie, using either the positive or the negative vocabulary words.

Journey to a World Without Words

STARDATE 74.14.04 CAPTAIN'S LOG: ARRIVED ON PLANET LINGULON-5 THIS MORNING. IT'S INHABITED BY A STRANGE GROUP OF HORSE-LIKE BEINGS CALLED LINGULOIDS. THE LINGULOIDS ARE A LOT LIKE EARTHLINGS— EXCEPT THEY HAVE POOR VOCABULARIES. TO SEE HOW POOR THEY ARE, READ THE ENTRIES BELOW.

Replace each underlined phrase with a single word from the list below.

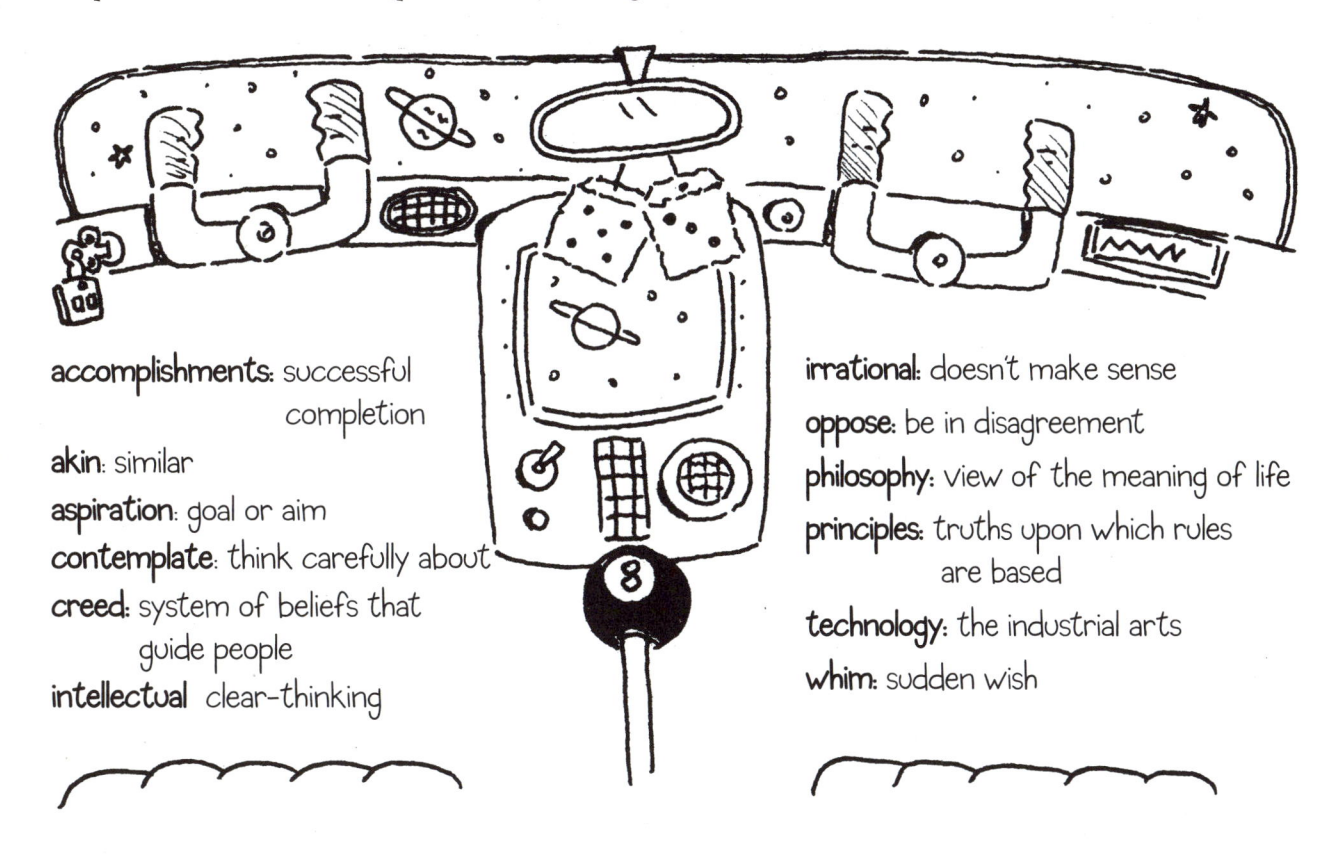

accomplishments: successful completion
akin: similar
aspiration: goal or aim
contemplate: think carefully about
creed: system of beliefs that guide people
intellectual clear-thinking

irrational: doesn't make sense
oppose: be in disagreement
philosophy: view of the meaning of life
principles: truths upon which rules are based
technology: the industrial arts
whim: sudden wish

1. A sign on the landing pad read: LINGULON-5 WELCOMES YOU. LINGULON-5 IS A NO-SMOKING PLANET THAT FEATURES BALMY BREEZES, SCENIC GOLF COURSES, AND GREAT SHOPPING. OUR ONLY <u>GOAL</u> _____ IS TO SATISFY YOUR EVERY <u>SUDDEN DESIRE</u> _____.

Name _____   **Date** _____

World Without Words

2. "Greetings, Earthlings," said Lingo-12. "You'll find that we Linguloids are <u>similar</u> _____ to you Earthlings—except for three things: (1) we have horse-like faces; (2) we eat peanut butter and hay sandwiches; and (3) our thought-processes are <u>not based on reason or logic</u> _____ And oh yes, a fourth thing—we wear diaper-like garments on top of our heads."

3. "Why do you wear diaper-like garments on top of your heads?" we asked. Lingo-12 replied, "We cannot answer that question because we are not thoughtful beings. We do not possess <u>great thinking</u> _____ skills. However, we do boast of many <u>successful efforts</u> _____ in the fields of golf and shopping."

4. Lingo-12 continued, "We invite you to visit our planet's scenic golf courses. Beings from as far as Romula come to play golf on Lingulon-5. Though we may <u>argue with</u> _____ the Romulans in our <u>view of life and wisdom</u> _____, we do agree about one thing: *Never use a 3-iron in a sand trap.*

5. "Because we only <u>think deeply about</u> _____ golf and shopping, our science and <u>industrial knowledge</u> _____ are underdeveloped. We have, for example, invented the wheel. But we put it to use only on golf carts," Lingo-12 explained.

6. Lingo-12 said, "Our <u>system of beliefs</u> _____ is simple. It is based on <u>basic, true ideas</u> _____. If something is good for golf or shopping, we believe in it. If it isn't good for golf or shopping, we don't believe in it."

GOING BEYOND

Write a final entry into the Captain's Log. Include a word that the Linguloids might not have. Then trade logs with a classmate. Define each other's new word.

Answer Key

Rowena and Squirmy in "Bicycle Power" (page 8)
1. b
2. a
3. a
4. c
5. a
6. six-sided figure
7. four-legged organism
8. thousand
9. million
10. many

Bill Klepper, Fat-Cat Wheeler-Dealer Billionaire (page 10)
1. atypical
2. disagree
3. ignoble
4. illiterate
5. imbalance
6. inexact
7. irresponsible
8. misinterpret
9. unpopular
10. coexist
11. condescend
12. correspond
13. symmetric
14. synthesis

Bill Klepper, Fat-Head Wheeler-Dealer Billionaire (page 12)
1. c
2. a
3. b
4. c
5. c
6. c
7. c
8. b
9. a
10. a
11. c
12. a
13. b
14. a

Sufferin' Suffixes (page 16)
1. acceptable
2. adaptation
3. heedless
4. clinician
5. defendant
6. wondrous
7. disdainful
8. delusional
9. entitlement
10. marriage
11. poetic
12. validate
13. digitize
14. inhibitor

The Word Machine (page 20)
1. inspect
2. expect
3. spectator
4. circumspect
5. prospect
6. perspective
7. respect
8. disrespectful
9. inspection
10. inspector

Professor Sylvia's Word Values (page 23)
1. transport, to carry from one place to another
2. importer, someone who sends items from one country to another
3. deportment, how you carry yourself
4. portable, able to carry easily

Ancient Latin Quizmo!!! (page 25)
1. injection
2. objective
3. subjective
4. projectile
5. inscribe
6. conscript
7. indescribable
8. conjecture, it means "a guess"

The Cutting Edge (page 27)
1. incisions
2. incisive
3. dissect
4. sector
5. precision
6. concise
7. excise
8. cross-section
9. decisive
10. intersect

11. The prefixes are ex and in. Excise means to "cut away from." Incisive means "cut clearly and sharply."
12. Trisect means to "cut into three pieces."
13. An incisor would be sharp because it means "to cut into." Possible animals: lion, tiger, dog, shark. Carnivores.

Nanette's Word Salon (page 29)
1. inverse
2. reverse
3. inversion, reversion
4. subvert
5. subversion
6. introvert
7. extrovert
8. controversy
9. controversial

Police Squad: MAU (Missing Affix Unit) (page 31)
1. telephones
2. television
3. televise
4. teleplay
5. telecommunications
6. telephoto
7. telecast
8. monologue
9. catalogue
10. dialogue
11. geophysicist
12. geological
13. geodes
14. geothermic
15. geography

Police Squad: SVU (Special Vocabulary Unit) (page 34)
1. animosity
2. skirmish
3. fracas
4. altercation
5. confrontation
6. trespass
7. felony
8. affront

Emily Taproot's Poetry Workshop (page 36)
1. a. entity, b. indifferent
2. c. dignified, d. mobile
3. e. discern, f. taciturn
4. g. rumor, h. devoid
5. i. Engage, j. microscopic
6. k. surmise, l. virtues
7. m. conviction
8. n. stout, o. ultimately, p. composed
9. q. chum, r. Eschew

Eddie Snively: World's Biggest Liar (page 38)
1. commend
2. conceive
3. coronation
4. galaxy
5. refute
6. categorically
7. triumph
8. convocation
9. prevaricating
10. allege
11. embossed
12. unaware
13. characterize
14. incidentally
15. assert
16. appellation
17. decorative
18. duplicity
19. relentless
20. outrage

Bingo Hackles, Sports Reporter (page 40)
1. reckoning
2. eliminated
3. fleet
4. proficiency
5. resumed
6. unquestionably
7. carom
8. plucked
9. transferred
10. descended
11. initiated
12. Fortunately
13. braced
14. thunderstruck
15. wavered
16. propelled
17. ascended
18. undoubtedly
19. radiates
20. locale

The Four Vocabularians: Dr. Dialect's Dictionary of Deception (page 42)
1. J
2. B
3. E
4. F
5. A
6. G
7. D
8. I
9. C
10. H

Laverne Weaselford, U.S. Senator (page 44)
1. righteous
2. submit
3. critical
4. federal
5. defame
6. Violators
7. incarceration
8. amend
9. prohibiting
10. candidates

Marla Murgatroid, Romance Novelist (page 45)
1. sultry
2. lounged
3. lustrous
4. gorgeous
5. prevailing
6. marvelous
7. sonorous
8. lithe
9. radiant
10. pounding
11. throb
12. unmistakable
13. dearest
14. stammered
15. cherish

Emily Taproot, Vocabulary Poet: The Language of Love (page 47)
1. phase
2. aloft
3. flitting
4. persistently
5. fragrance
6. efface
7. grizzled
8. expeditiously
9. embrace
10. discretion
11. tenacious
12. inconspicuous
13. pungent
14. interface
15. hurtling
16. relinquish
17. debase
18. ludicrous
19. contorting
20. flawless

The Four Vocabularians: The National Word Day Speech (page 49)
1. citizens, budget
2. revenue, sufficient
3. grave, predicament
4. regret, jeopardy
5. inessential, illegitimate
6. pledge, salvage
7. penalize, redundant
8. generate, festivities
9. conclude, entreat

The Wordies (page 51)
1. C
2. E
3. A
4. B
5. D
6. trying to be funny, often at the wrong time
7. being funny by saying the opposite of what one means
8. making fun of others in a mean way
9. stupid, silly, or foolish
10. light-hearted and gentle humor
11. B
12. D
13. A
14. C

Buck Bickley's Big Braggin' Book (page 53)
1. denomination
2. elite
3. perilous
4. modest
5. resplendently
6. distinct
7. keen
8. polygot
9. penetrating
10. affluent

11. expansive
12. disperse
13. candid
14. droll
15. violation

Buck Bickley's Dog's Big Braggin' Book (page 55)
1. prosperous, retrieve
2. pursue, frequently
3. shrewd, compassionate
4. amiable, secluded
5. peerless, ideal

Julie Kablooie's Hollywood Gossip Column (page 56)
1. a
2. c
3. b
4. b
5. c
6. c
7. c
8. a

Do You Have What it Takes to Become a Freelance Know-It-All Reviewer? (page 57)
Answers will vary

Journey to a World Without Words (page 59)
1. aspiration, whim
2. akin, irrational
3. intellectual, accomplishments
4. oppose, philosophy
5. contemplate, technology
6. creed, principles